RIANNE OAKWOOD

MAKE IT STICK

The Ultimate Guide on How You Can Achieve Your Goals, Learn How to Master the Art of Goal Setting And Establishing Self-Discipline So You Can Achieve Your Dreams

Descrierea CIP a Bibliotecii Naţionale a României
RIANNE OAKWOOD
    MAKE IT STICK. The Ultimate Guide on How You Can Achieve Your Goals, Learn How to Master the Art of Goal Setting And Establishing Self-Discipline So You Can Achieve Your Dreams / Rianne Oakwood. – Bucharest: Editura My Ebook, 2020
    ISBN

RIANNE OAKWOOD

MAKE IT STICK

The Ultimate Guide on How You Can Achieve Your Goals, Learn How to Master the Art of Goal Setting And Establishing Self-Discipline So You Can Achieve Your Dreams

My Ebook Publishing House
Bucharest, 2020

CONTENTS

Introduction ………………………………………..   7

This Book Will Teach You The Following ……………..   10

Chapter 1 – **Figuring Out Which Goals To Set** …………   15

What Do You Need to Do to Achieve These Objectives?...   16

What Could Go Wrong? ……………………………   18

Figuring Out Your Goals ……………………………   20

Set Realistic Goals ……………………………………   20

Chapter 2 – **Set More Effective Goals By Incorporating**

            Discipline - Building Elements …………………   24

Prioritize Your Sub-goals ……………………………   24

Be as Clear About Your Sub-goals' Parts as Possible ………   25

Build Discipline by Making Your Highest Priority

Sub-goal Your Primary Focus ………………………   26

Chapter 3 – **Use Daily Rituals to Fine Tune and Achieve Your Goals** 28

Physical Rituals 29

Why Do Physical Rituals Work? 30

Mental Rituals Start Your Day Right 31

Pre-task Mental Rituals 34

Pre-sleep Ritual 36

Chapter 4 – **Measure Your Success to Boost Your Motivation** 38

Compare Yourself To Your Ideal Self In The Here And Now   40

Chapter 5 – **Learn When To Scale Up** 41

The Optimal Way To Scale Up 42

Execute. Implement. Do it today 43

Conclusion 46

INTRODUCTION

Hello and welcome to our short, beginners guide on mastering the art of setting goals & establishing self-discipline

Discipline, I'm afraid to report, is crucial for any success in life. Success, in whatever field or area of life, requires five things. You need to wait for it, you have to persevere through the many different challenges and setbacks you are bound to encounter.

You also have to put in constant effort. Success usually doesn't happen the first time you try. In fact, in many situations, it requires several tries. You have to constantly put in the effort.

Finally, success requires putting up with adverse conditions. You have to keep at it regardless of what you're feeling, regardless of how many people discourage you, and regardless of whether you feel that it's time or not. You have to do it.

Success requires all of these and these all involve discipline. So what's the problem? I'm sure it's quite obvious. Modern life and values aren't exactly very friendly towards discipline. In fact, our modern world and the principles behind it seem to actively work against self-discipline.

First of all, we want everything to be quick and easy. I'm not just talking about products and services, I'm talking about relationships. I'm talking about education. It's as if we've developed a sense of entitlement that life has to be fair, quick and easy.

Given this reality and these principles, it is no surprise that our attention span collectively has shrunk dramatically. And it's continuing to shrink. You only need to ask the nearest Millenial to know what I'm talking about.

People's time horizon, as far as the "good things in life" are concerned, is very short. People don't have the time nor the patience. They definitely don't have the discipline to wait around, deal with all sorts of adverse conditions, and put in constant work.

They definitely don't have the patience to stick with trying situations until the thing that they're working on pans out.

Unfortunately, if you want to achieve success, you need to set up goals properly and pursue those goals. You can hope and

8

wish all you want, but big victories in your life are not going to materialize out of sheer luck. You have to plan them out and you have to work your plan. In other words, you have to set goals and implement them. Again, there goes that word: discipline is required.

Self-discipline is essential, but effective goal setting also requires clarity of purpose, proper structuring of your goals, and finally, proper measurement of your success. If you're able to do all of these and you have the proper level of self-discipline, success becomes a habit.

Have you ever hung out with people who make a tremendous amount of money seemingly effortlessly? Have you hung out with people who declare their big plans and the next time you check with them or check with people who know them, those plans panned out?

Well, those people are not magical, I'm sorry to report. Those people are not some sort of mystical alien creature race. No. They simply picked up on the right habits. Simply put, people who succeed easily just make it look easy.

Believe it or not, it took a lot of falls, stumbles, overcoming doubts, challenges as well as potential humiliation to get to where they are now. The good news? Success is a habit that can be learned.

Now I know you might be thinking that successful people look, behave and sound so different from you. You might even be thinking that they are a completely different race of people. Well, don't let appearances fool you. On the surface, it may seem like they're completely different from you, but understand that they're just working out of certain habits. You don't have to be born with those habits. You don't have to be lucky. You just need to commit to learning it.

This Book Will Teach You The Following

To help you travel the road to success and greater self-discipline, this book will teach you the following. First, you will learn to figure out which goals to set. Believe it or not, the goals you select do have an impact on the success you achieve.

Many people fail to achieve the kind of results they're looking for, simply because they set their eyes and their minds on the wrong set of goals. Now, those goals may be perfect for other people, but it's not right for them. Try as hard as they might, nothing seems to work. And it can be traced to the fact that they picked the wrong goals to set.

Second, you're going to learn how to set more effective goals by incorporating discipline-building elements. A lot of people set up goals in such a way that these goals suck up all available willpower they may bring to the table. In other words, there's no built-in incentive or self-sustaining system in the goals. The goals just take, take and take.

Now, it doesn't take a scientist to figure out that with such goals, it's too easy to hit a wall. It's too easy to think that you're trying so hard and putting in so much time and effort and nothing seems to work. When you find yourself in that space, it's not that difficult to start believing that you're just not cut out for success. It's very easy to get discouraged, and eventually, you give up.

As you probably already know, the only way to fail at anything in life is to quit. And that's precisely what you're setting yourself up for if you don't know how to set up goals to be self-sustaining. At the very least, they have to be self-sustaining in terms of your discipline.

Third, I'm going to teach you how to use daily rituals to fine tune and achieve your goals. You have to understand that people are what they consistently do. People can talk a good game, other people might have all sorts of mistaken notions about them, however, their real character boils down to what they consistently do. In other words, it's all about their rituals.

Believe it or not, you already have a set of rituals. You may not be aware of them, but they exist. What if I told you that you could be achieving more with your life if you only chose to be a little bit more conscious of the rituals you engage in? These rituals have a direct and immediate impact on your performance on many different levels. At the very least, they can help or slow down the achievement of your goals.

Another thing that I will help you with involves measuring success. A lot of people sabotage themselves because they choose to measure their success in the wrong way. Now, it's okay to measure your success in terms of ultimate measurements. For example, if you're just starting a business, it's okay to think from time to time about the millions of dollars you could be making.

However, if you choose to only use ultimate measurements of success, you are just setting yourself up to lose your drive, motivation and passion in the here and now. Don't be surprised if you get so discouraged and demotivated that you just give up.

Sadly, people do this all the time.

Finally, I will teach you about the signals you need to pay attention to that will clear you to scale up. Please understand that if you want to achieve any kind of success, you cannot stay at the same level. You might be doing things really well at that level, people might talk highly of you, but if you stay at that level and you allow your comfort zone to define what is possible for you, you're going to get stuck.

You might have started the process with all these hopes and dreams and grand visions, but let me tell you, they will all remain stuck in your head. Your waking reality is not going to measure up because you refuse to scale up. I'll teach you how to do that.

More precisely, I'll teach you to detect the signals that would enable you to scale up.

Are you ready to begin?...

Let's dive in!

CHAPTER 1

FIGURING OUT WHICH GOALS TO SET

First things first, be clear as to what your big objectives in life are. What are your ultimate objectives in life? Do you want to travel the world? Do you want to build a legacy in the form of a company or an organization or school? Do you want to help a lot of people in the form of a charity? What are your big objectives in life?

Now, keep in mind that since this is personal in nature, there is really no such thing as a right or wrong answer. One person's big objective is no better or worse than somebody else's. After all, we come from different backgrounds and different families. We have different values and we definitely have different experiences. And all these differences add up to the way we look at the world and the way we choose our objectives. Focus on what objective makes most sense in your life and focus on the big ones.

What Do You Need to Do to Achieve These Objectives?

Now that you're clear as to what your big objectives are in life - and you shouldn't hold yourself back when thinking these up - the next thing to think about is what you need to do. What kind of actions do you need to take to make these objectives a reality?

You probably already know that you can't just simply hope and wish your objectives to materialize. The law of attraction does work, but it only works when there is action involved. You can't simply just mentally imagine certain things happening and refuse to lift a finger. Don't be surprised if nothing happens when you refuse to lift a finger.

There has to be some sort of objective change in the way you think as well as the way you talk and act for your desired reality to happen. Accordingly, focus on what you need to do to achieve these objectives.

I started you off with the big objectives in your life because I want you to get pumped up about the ultimate reward. When you look at the big rewards at the end, you can then start tracing back to where you are today. If your ultimate objective is to live in a $10 million mansion in the nice part of town, start with the vision of you living in that mansion. Allow yourself to feel good.

Allow yourself to feel pumped up and excited about that reality.

Next, start tracing back in terms of the actions you took from that point to where you are now. You need to do this so you can remain focused on the big objective and maintain the right level of motivation. However, more importantly, you need to do this backwards progression to create a map in your mind. You end up seeing the clear logical conclusion between the things you need to do in the here and now to achieve a certain future.

While we could have easily projected from now to the future, you're more likely to get pumped up and excited when we start the discussion with the reward first. Regardless of how you do it, you should have a rough idea of the clear logical conclusion between the things that you need to do now and the kind of life you could be enjoying in the future.

What Could Go Wrong?

Now that I have taught you about focusing on your ultimate objectives first and then tracing back, what's the point? Couldn't you just have done it the same way, but projecting from now to the future?

Well, you could do that. And that's exactly how many people choose to go about it. The problem is, they end up going around in circles. They really do. It's as if they're just chasing their tails. Day in, day out, they put in all sorts of effort, they try to focus, but nothing seems to happen because they just end up where they began.

The reason for this is they lack purpose. The idea that they have seems so fuzzy because it's projected into the future. It's too easy for them to get sucked up by the trials and tribulations of their life in the here and now. In fact, if you ask a lot of people who are working hard for a "future," many of them simply lack purpose. They really do.

They know that they need to make a change, but they don't know what kind of change. They know that they want a good future for them or "more money" or more opportunities, but they can't quite put their finger on it. This lack of clarity and ultimate
18

purpose clouds people's goal setting activities. They lack a clear view of why. It is no surprise then that even if they know what to do or how to do it, nothing seems to work. At the very least, they're settling for mediocrity.

The reason for this is simple. Without a clear view of "why," it wouldn't matter if you know what to do or how to do it. You have to focus on purpose. Is your purpose strong enough to push you through all the hassles, challenges and setbacks you are bound to encounter? Is your purpose appealing enough so that you would want to change and overcome your negative mental and emotional habits that get in the way? That's how important purpose is, and this is why I taught you to focus on your big objectives in life first.

Clarify them. Make them as vivid in your mind as possible. Allow them to pump you up and get you excited. Once you have that bright beacon long into the future or at the farthest end of possibility, you then trace back to where you are now. If you trace back realistically, you create not just a direct logical connection between your objectives and your excitement now, but you also create a map on how to get there.

Figuring Out Your Goals

This backward progression enables you to establish three big things. You figure your big objectives, you become aware of goals that lead to these big objectives, and you also would be able to break down these goals into sub-goals that you can do in the here and now. In other words, you get a realistic mind map that will enable you to get from Point A to Point B. You get a clear and actionable bridge from how things are, to what you would like them to be.

This is an exercise in your ability to change and impact your material reality. This is not an empty exercise. This is not just intellectual speculation. This is real.

Set Realistic Goals

Now, it's very easy to get taken in by your big objectives. It's very easy to think that somehow, some way, you will come up with the right thing at the right time to impress the right people so the right things happen in your life. Unfortunately, nobody's that lucky.

For every mention of the word "right," there's a lot of work that needs to be done. A lot of things need to fall into place. And to automatically assume that these things would just happen simply involves an all-abiding belief in luck. Again, nobody's that lucky. It's like asking to be struck by lightning several times at the same spot, at the same time.

The better approach is to look at the goals between your life as it exists now and the ideal life that you see for yourself in the future. Understand that those goals that get you from here to there aren't just composed of one unchangeable set of goals.

There are many alternative goals that provide the stepping stones that enable you to get from here to there.

Since you have a choice of different goals, your job right now is to figure out which goals are the most realistic. How do you wrap your mind around this? How do you make sense of this? Well, very simple. You apply the following five filters.

You ask yourself whether these goals can be supported by the resources you currently have right now or the resources you can realistically build up. Maybe you can take out a loan, maybe you can get a job, or maybe you can get a second job. Maybe friends and family can help you. Whatever the case may be, don't just focus on the resources you have right now, but also focus on resources that you realistically can quickly get access to.

Next, you have to filter your goals based on whether they truly fit your personal passion or personality. Now, don't be disappointed if you're not currently passionate about something or something doesn't fit your personality now. You might fall in love with it later. You might get used to it. Your mindset might change. If that is a realistic possibility, then your goal can still be realistic.

The third filter that you need to apply is whether the goal can be broken down into smaller sub-goals. This is crucial. If a goal cannot be broken down into smaller parts that can be achieved in the here and now or within a reasonable period of time, with existing or attainable resources, then you have a problem on your hands. Chances are, you're just hoping and wishing. You're probably just daydreaming. Do yourself a big favor and make sure that the goals can actually be broken down into sub-goals that you can take action on or implement right here, right now or with minimal changes.

Next, you have to make sure that the goals that you are pursuing can be placed on a timeline. You know you have a problem on your hands if the goal obviously will take forever or has no fixed start date. Make sure that you can put it on a timeline. Your timeline is not just a set of annoying deadlines, but instead, it's actually a measurement of how realistic your goal is.

Oftentimes, the big difference between a realistic and an unrealistic goal is that realistic goals can be scheduled. If you show up at the right place at the right time to do the right things, you achieve your goal. Do that enough times and you get closer and closer to your big objective. If that's not possible with your goal, you might be looking at something that's unrealistic.

Finally, you need to make sure that when picking among alternative goals that take you from where you are now to where you would like to be, these must be measurable in terms of attainment as well as the quality of success. If you feel that the achievement of these goals is very easy, and pretty much any effort gets you there, then you might not actually be working with realistic goals. You might be disappointed with the results because it may well turn out that it doesn't really get you to where you need to go.

CHAPTER 2

SET MORE EFFECTIVE GOALS BY INCORPORATING DISCIPLINE-BUILDING ELEMENTS

What if I told you that you can set up your goals in such a way that they can be self-sustaining? In other words, they train you to become more disciplined. And the more you achieve these goals, the more disciplined you become and you are able to take on more and more goals. Sounds awesome, right? Well, this is not theory. It can happen and people do make it happen. Here's how you do it.

Prioritize Your Sub-goals

The first thing that you need to do is to prioritize the sub-goals or sub-elements of your big goals. You sort them based on their likelihood to lead to big objectives. In other words, if you knock out these sub-goals, they directly take you closer to your big objectives.

Of course, not all sub-goals are like this. Sometimes, sub-goals are necessary, but they lead to an indirect path. As long as you're reasonably certain that if you take that indirect path it eventually leads you to your big goals, then that sub-goal is good enough.

List down all these sub-goals and make it your highest priority to focus on sub-goals that are the most directly connected to your big objectives. In other words, when you do these sub-goals, it's like going from Point A to Point B. The shorter and the straighter the line, the better.

Be as Clear About Your Sub-goals' Parts as Possible

While prioritizing sub-goals is important, you also need to make sure that you conceptualize them correctly. Look at the sub-goals' parts and make sure that you're clear as to what you need to do, how to do it, when to do it, and where to do it. The most important ingredient, of course, is to be clear as to why you're doing this sub-goal.

What is its impact on your big objectives? How does it get you there? What kind of role does it play in helping you achieve the big things that you're shooting for in your life?

Build Discipline by Making Your Highest Priority Sub-goal Your Primary Focus

In every given day, make sure that you are focusing on sub-goals that lead you closer to your big objectives. Make these sub-goals and their activities your primary focus. Everything must lead to it. Keep this top of mind. Also, make it a point to do the hardest part of these sub-goals first.

Make no mistake about it, regardless of sub-goal or set of activities, there's always something that you're going to struggle with. There's always going to be a part of a project that you have a tough time starting. Maybe it's technically easy, but you're just emotionally intimidated by it. On the other hand, it may be emotionally easy and very straightforward as far as your understanding of its necessity is concerned, but it's technically challenging for you. Regardless, zero in on these hardest parts and choose to do them first.

I know it won't be easy. At first, it's probably going to feel like you're pulling teeth. It's definitely not going to happen overnight. However, the more you keep at it, the greater your self-discipline becomes because you're tackling the hardest thing first. You're not running away from it, you're not procrastinating, you're not trying to work around it, but you're tackling it head on. Sure, the first attack is probably going to be very brutal, but the more you keep attacking, the more confident you become. At the very least, you're not intimidated.

Keep this up and this can lead to you taking consistent action that ensures your sub-goals are achieved. The more sub-goals you knock out, of course, the closer you get to your big objectives.

This is not exactly rocket science or brain surgery.

CHAPTER 3

USE DAILY RITUALS TO FINE TUNE
AND ACHIEVE YOUR GOALS

Let's get one thing clear here, as clear as you may get on the sub-goals that you need to do each and every day, and as pumped up as you may be now, please understand that success is a long-haul journey. It really is. It's a marathon. It's not one of those things that you just choose to do now and somehow, some way, things would just fall into place.

It doesn't work that way. Things sometimes pan out this way, but it doesn't happen all the time. You definitely can't bank on it. This is where your daily rituals come in.

Everybody has rituals. The problem is, for the most part, our rituals are either neutral and don't really help us either way, or they work against us. By being a little bit more mindful and purposeful regarding the daily rituals you carry out, you can well position yourself for greater and greater levels of success. You also position yourself for increasing levels of self-discipline.

These two concepts coincide in the form of the rituals you choose. Daily rituals come in four different types: physical, mental, mental rituals before tasks, and rituals you engage in before you sleep. You have to be conscious about all of these so you can make them work for you instead of having them work against you.

Physical Rituals

Physical rituals involve things that you physically do every day on a consistent basis. These are very important because they center you. Your mind and body can be aligned or can be misaligned, depending on your physical rituals.

If your ritual is to watch TV for three hours straight, then that's going to have an impact on your life, whether you like it or not. If you choose to jog every morning or workout at the gym hitting the weights three times a week, that's going to have an impact on your life, again, whether you like it or not.

Focus on the physical resetting quality of physical rituals. Look for rituals that maximize this sense of physical reset where you feel that you're getting a fresh start. At the very least, aim for physical rituals that give you some sort of mental clarity.

Usually, people use physical rituals involving daily exercise, timing their meals, wake up time, or taking cold showers. You might be thinking that taking a cold shower is a form of self- punishment, but you'd be wrong. When you take a cold shower, your mind doesn't wander. You force yourself to act efficiently because you don't want to freeze. You also start thinking in a very focused way. You'd be surprised as to how long this focused thinking will linger as your day goes on.

Why Do Physical Rituals Work?

The bottom line is that physical rituals produce positive results because of the positive association you create. When you engage in a physical ritual, like daily exercise or taking ice cold showers, you focus. It's hard to do weight training in an unfocused way - you're going to spend an eternity in the gym. If you workout correctly, you're forced to focus. The same applies to taking a cold shower.

This is personal productivity dynamite because you only need to engage in the physical ritual and your body will automatically supply the focus. Why? It already developed a tight association between the level of mental, emotional and spiritual awareness of the moment you're in that you achieve with certain physical stimuli like an ice-cold shower. You only need to subject yourself to that physical stimuli for your mind to kick in.

Mental Rituals To Start Your Day Right

You need to adopt mental rituals that start your day on an optimal level. You really do. While physical rituals do a great job of resetting your willpower, focus and mental energy, you can't just rely on these rituals. You should also be more proactive as far as your mental activities are concerned. This is why I would suggest that you practice feeling grateful the first thing in the morning.

The first few minutes of your waking consciousness every morning should involve you thinking about how lucky you are. Think about how you've been blessed to sleep through the night. Think about how fortunate you are to have food in your belly, a roof over your head, and nobody sneaking up behind you to plunge a knife into your neck. I know that sounds far-fetched to a lot of people, but you'd be surprised as to how many things you take for granted.

Feel fortunate that you don't have stage four brain cancer. Feel grateful for the fact that you're able to breathe comfortably without pain or the need for medication. There are just so many things that you can feel grateful for.

Why do this? Well, when you feel grateful for something, you humble your mind. You really do. You quiet it. It's no longer about what you need. It's no longer about whether life is fair or unfair to you. Instead, when you allow yourself to feel grateful, you become other-centered. You focus on the objective world, and your relationship to the world then becomes healthier.

Consider the flip side. You can choose to be so self-centered that you eventually trick yourself into feeling that the world revolves around you. You might think that that is a very self-empowering way of thinking, but it actually leads to a dead end.

If you think that the world revolves around you, then you would become overly sensitive. Everything is a judgment of you. If people aren't nice to you, then it's all about you. Maybe they're just having a bad time. Maybe they're just going through some rough situations in their life. It's not about you. They're just projecting, and you're not necessarily the target.

But unfortunately, if your main focus is on yourself and you're extremely self-absorbed, you become so touchy that you end up limiting your success. You become easily discouraged because life is unfair. You become frustrated because things don't flow easily as you imagined they should.

Feel grateful. Allow yourself to feel humble and suppress that ego.

Next, practice affirmations. Celebrate things that you do right. Celebrate what you have to offer. Be aware of your competence and the value you bring to other people's lives. When you practice affirmations, you build your confidence. You reshape your ego into a more positive form that would enable you to achieve more.

Usually, we let our egos thwart our success by unrealistically shaping our expectations. When you practice affirmations, you're in full control of how you would like your ego to perceive your capabilities and personal possibilities.

Pre-task Mental Rituals

Before you roll up your sleeves and get down to business, as far as work or school is concerned, engage in these rituals. They do an amazing job of clearing up any mental obstacles or emotional hurdles that degrade your effectiveness.

First, practice deep breathing. What if I told you that by simply breathing deeply and slowly 8 to 10 times, you clear your mind and you energize your body?

Next, engage in some sort of mental cleansing. This doesn't have to be anything fancy. You basically just refuse to hang onto negative thoughts. Refuse to get worked up over an issue that you really can't control. Maybe there's just something that you're struggling with from yesterday, while this morning, choose to let that go.

Once you've done mental cleansing, the next step is to mentally cleanse yourself as far as the task in front of you is concerned. Focus on what you know about the task and don't leave anything to judgment. Just focus on the mechanics of the task. Don't over analyze it, don't pre-judge it, don't dismiss it as either too hard or impossible or beneath you. Instead, just look at it as a series of technical instructions. Keep only these things in your mind.

Technical instructions should be the only thing in your mental databanks.

Next, start the task. This is crucial. Just decide when to start and don't give yourself any excuses to not start. For example, if you decide to hit the books at 8 AM, do exactly that when the time comes. No more, no less. Don't give yourself excuses, don't blame other people, don't make justifications, don't bargain with yourself. Stop engaging in any of that internal shenanigans and jump in with both feet and get down to business.

After you've started, race through the task. This is very important. A lot of people are clueless about this. You have to understand that it's very easy for our work or academic activities to become time rabbit holes. Seriously.

You jump in, and you can't get out because it just sucks you in. There's just so many chambers. There are so many directions you can go, and by the time you realize it, time's up.

Start your task by focusing like a laser on what you need to do. It has to be a small, narrow range of activities. Once you've started the task, race through the task. In other words, play a game with yourself. Pretend you're in a marathon and you're basically knocking out all these tasks as quickly as possible.

It's important, however, to race, but to go through a quality checklist. You're not looking to cut corners, you're not looking to compromise quality. Your objective is to race through the task, while at the same time, making sure that the output that you produce meets quality standards. This is very important because the more you do this and the more you get used to it, the more likely you will master that task. Eventually, you would reach a point where it becomes easy or second nature to you.

Finally, take small breaks, but stick to schedule. For example, if you allow yourself 3-minute breaks after big productivity tasks, stick to that. After the break period is over, start the race again.

Pre-sleep Ritual

Before you sleep, make sure that you adopt these rituals or something similar to them. Whatever the case may be, adopt rituals that achieve the same objectives.

First, write down your goals for the next day. This is very important because you are able to mentally map out what you expect from yourself the following day. When you do this, you're no longer blindsided by the task you'll be doing the next day.

You're no longer emotionally intimidated. Instead, you're mentally focused as to the grand objectives you need to knock out.

Next, once you have your list going, mentally rehearse what it would feel like to successfully achieve those goals. Imagine yourself doing the work, having a good time, and then achieving success at the end of the sub-goal. Allow yourself to feel good.

Let the sense of accomplishment sink in.

After that, think about your big objectives or your big goals. Imagine how it would feel to achieve them. This way, you feel pumped up sufficiently so when you're knocking out your sub- goals, you don't feel that what you're doing is pointless. You feel driven, you feel purposeful, and this enables you to do the right things at the right time to produce the right amount of value.

CHAPTER 4

MEASURE YOUR SUCCESS
TO BOOST YOUR MOTIVATION

As I have mentioned in the introduction of this book, a lot of people insist on measuring their success in the most negative way possible. They may just be starting their relationship, their business, or their schooling, but they're already measuring themselves based on ultimate objectives.

For example, if you've just started a small business and you start measuring yourself based on how many millions of dollars you're making, you probably are going to achieve one thing and one thing alone: making yourself miserable. Keep that up and you shouldn't be surprised if you eventually quit. You might eventually conclude that you're chasing a pipe dream. It's not going to happen because you're not getting the results that you are looking for. In your mind, you're not achieving the success that you set out to get.

The problem, however, is not the goal. The problem is not the business. The problem is not your activities, but your mindset.

You insisted on measuring your success using an inappropriate measurement.

Make no mistake about it, your measurement of success can hobble you. Don't expect ultimate success before its time. Don't destroy your motivation levels.

You're pumped up right now. You're on a mission. You want to do certain things. You're excited about your big objectives. Don't screw all that up by whipping out a measuring tape that uses ultimate objective results. Instead, focus on measuring your success based on where you are.

For example, if you just started a business, focus on measuring success based on whether you have filed the right permits, whether you bought the furniture or gotten the right equipment and set up the right protocol for your office. In other words, focus on realistic success metrics instead of ultimate ones.

I'm not saying that you should lower the bar. I'm not saying you should forget about ultimately making money. I'm not saying that at all. Instead, I'm telling you to focus on what makes the most sense to your venture right here, right now.

Compare Yourself To Your Ideal Self In The Here And Now

If you really want to optimize your success, make sure you compare yourself now to your ideal self. Your ideal successful self has a certain amount of habits. This person has certain standards. This person works a certain way. Knowing that, what do you stand to learn? What changes can you make in the here and now to live up to your ideal self?

This is extremely important because when you do this, you aim to meet the highest level of quality. You're less likely to quit. You're also less likely to feel frustrated. After all, your role model is your ideal self. This is the version of you that performs at peak levels.

Use this to inspire you. You might not get there, you might not be able to achieve the same high level precisely, but at the very least, you're motivated enough to put in more effort than you would normally do otherwise.

CHAPTER 5

LEARN WHEN TO SCALE UP

If you've followed all the tips above, you would be able to do a task every single day, regardless of whether you feel like it or not. You would be able to put one foot in front of the other, regardless of how tired you were from the previous day.

Congratulations. You are able to commit, you are able to put in the work. This ensures ultimate success if you keep it up long enough.

Now, with that said, please understand that you have to scale up. You can't stay where you are. You can't focus on the tried and proven and resolve to gain all your security from it. You have to push yourself to go up and out. You have to constantly push yourself to go to the next level.

Unfortunately, people don't scale up. They just focus on what's easy to them and leave it at that. This leads to failure again and again. Why? Eventually, their skills decline. They don't put in the time or effort to know what they need to learn so they can do a better job or so they can provide better value to other people. They just focus on what they need right here, right now.

As good as you are, eventually, this mindset is not going to enable you to achieve your big objectives. You're clinging too tightly to your comfort zone.

Understand that you have to scale up. You have to produce more, you have to give more value, and you have to otherwise have a more positive impact. You can't just focus on doing a good job and settling for good enough. You have to focus on becoming the very best you can be.

So how exactly do you scale up? How do you get closer and closer to the very best version of you? Well, it's actually quite easy.

The Optimal Way To Scale Up

To scale up in a systematic and methodical way, you just need to first implement your idea. Just take action. You have a plan, you have a clear understanding of what you need to do, just do it.

Implement. Execute.

This might seem straightforward, but you'd be surprised as to how many people screw this up. They think about all sorts of amazing possibilities, they allow themselves to feel good about how smart they are because they can think about all these things, but they refuse to take action. They find excuse after excuse or, worse yet, they blame other people, and the end result is the same. They don't take any action. Their hopes and dreams remain far and distant.

Execute. Implement. Do it today.

Next, once you've taken action, you know whether you are getting the maximum amount of results and the highest quality that you could hope for. You'd be blind to be clueless regarding this. If you take a look at the results that you're getting with unvarnished eyes, you would know and admit that there is room for improvement.

This is where you fine tune. You try to tighten things up. You try to polish your performance so that it's as good as it could be.

However, there will be certain areas that need more effort from you. This brings us to the next step: Innovation.

Understand that with everything else being equal, you are probably on the same level as everybody else you're competing with at a job or in your business. For you to stand out head and shoulders from them, you need to innovate. You need to look at common problems you encounter and come up with something that would save time and resources or produce better quality.

If you're able to do this, things become easier. Once things become easy, make sure you explore other parts of the tasks to truly master. Once you reach the stage where you know everything like the back of your hand, or you can do things while you're sleeping, this is when you scale up.

Either you boost the number of things that you do or you increase the quality standards of your work. Whatever the case may be, scaling up involves producing more value. If you scale up in a systematic and methodical way, and you're able to do this consistently, you will achieve success sooner rather than later.

What Does Mastery Mean?

To recap, mastery boils down to increasing speed or increasing quality. Eventually, once you have taken care of speed and quality, you must actively work at boosting both of them at the same time. That's how you produce solid results consistently.

CONCLUSION

Congratulations on making it to the end of this short, introductory guide on mastering the art of goal setting and building self discipline.

You may be surprised to know that the majority of people who start something never complete it.

Take your time and progress at your own pace. This is not a race. The more you understand and comprehend about building the discipline needed to achieve the goals you set the better.

If you really want to succeed, then everything you do for your life must be with long-term planning in mind. These changes you're making are not meant to be temporary. They're meant to be part of a new lifestyle that you follow.

You can't think of self-discipline as simply as something that you add into your day once or twice a week. Setting better goals and achieving them, must instead be something that your life is about all the time...and only then can you truly reap the benefits of being self-disciplined

Set the right goals and you will achieve the success you feel you deserve in life. Pick the wrong goals or have the wrong game plan in achieving those goals and you will continue to get the same results as everybody else. That's right, you're going to continue to struggle.

Please understand that successful people are not different from you. They did not come from some sort of alien or foreign planet. They simply did not get lucky. They were definitely not bred to be that successful. Instead, they're just like you. They learned things. They learned to focus on certain things. That's the big difference between them and you.

If they can do it, you can do it too. It's all about learned behavior.

The tips and tricks that I've outlined in this book give you a place to start in learning the things that you need to take your life to the highest level. Stop being frustrated about the kind of life you could have been living. Stop comparing yourself to other people who seem to be more successful than you. Instead, focus on what you can do in the here and now.

By reading this information and incorporating them and taking action on them day after day, eventually, you will get to where you need to go. The only person holding you back from the life of relentless and continuous victory you were born to achieve is you. Are you going to choose success today? Only you can answer that question.

I wish you all the success with making goal setting & self-discipline part of your daily life.

Printed by Libri Plureos GmbH in Hamburg, Germany